ERIC BAUMGARTNER'S

JAZZ IT·UP!

SERIES

MID-INTERMEDIATE PIANO SOLO

CLASSICS

ISBN 978-1-4234-7772-3

WILLIS MUSIC

EXCLUSIVELY DISTRIBUTED BY

HAL•LEONARD®
CORPORATION
7777 W. BLUEMOUND RD. P.O. BOX 13819
MILWAUKEE, WISCONSIN 53213

Visit Hal Leonard Online at
www.halleonard.com

Habanera
from *Carmen*

Georges Bizet (1838–1875)
Arranged by Eric Baumgartner

TRACKS
1–2

Smooth and mysterious

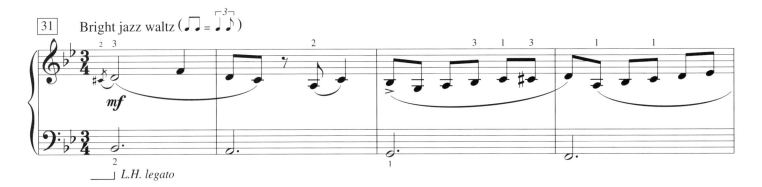

Bright jazz waltz

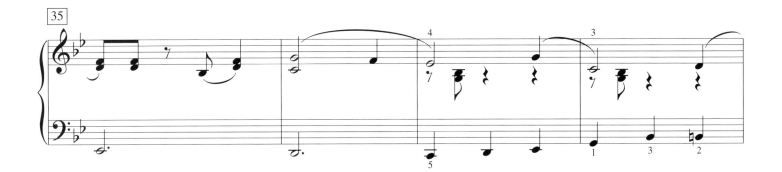

L.H. legato

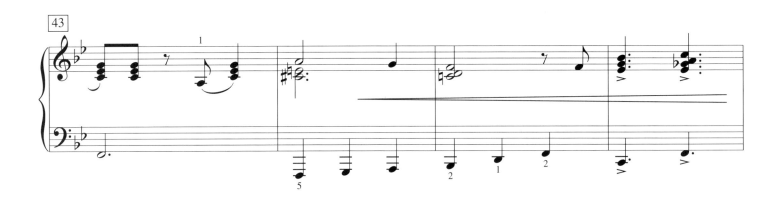

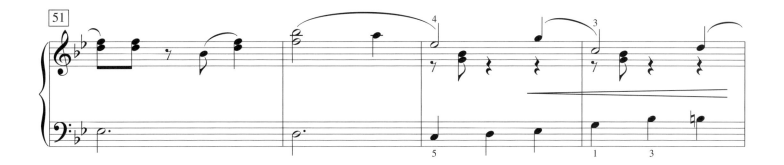

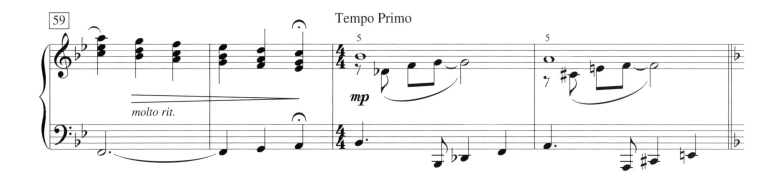

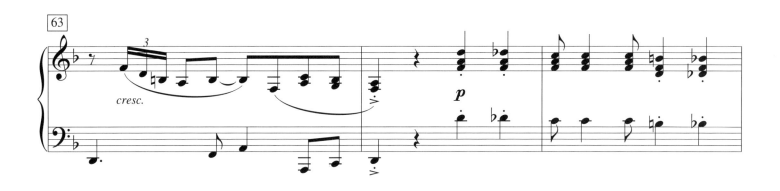

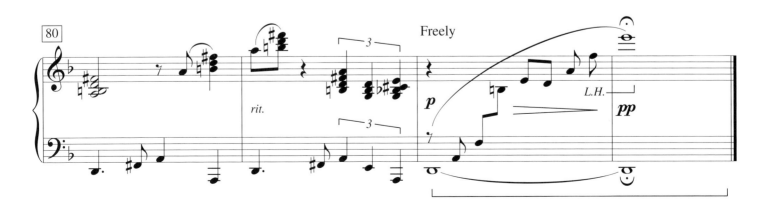

Sugar Plum Funk

Pyotr Il'yich Tchaikovsky (1840–1893)
Arranged by Eric Baumgartner

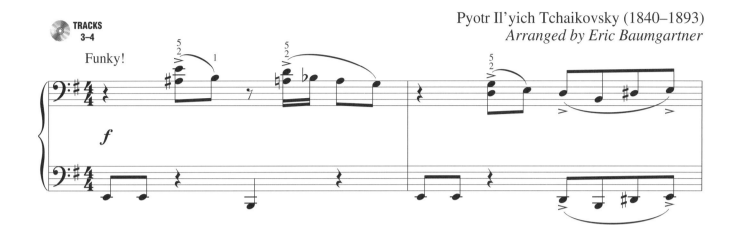

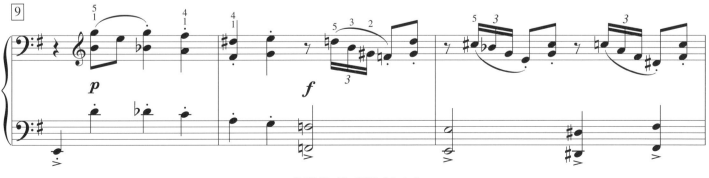

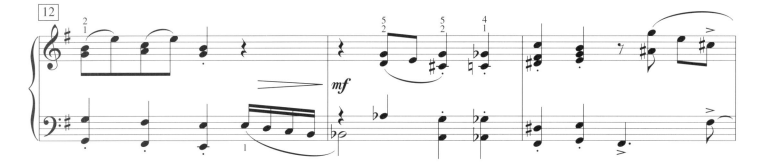

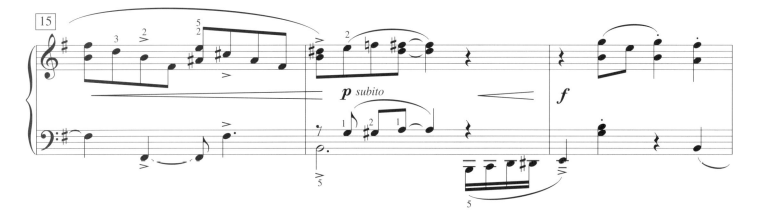

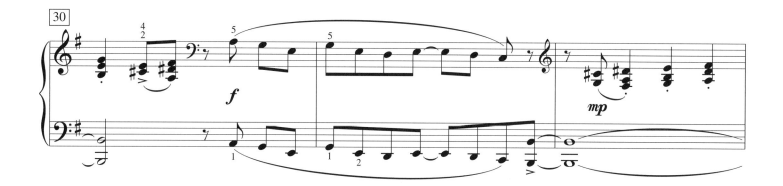

Funeral March of a Marionette

Charles Gounod (1818–1893)
Arranged by Eric Baumgartner

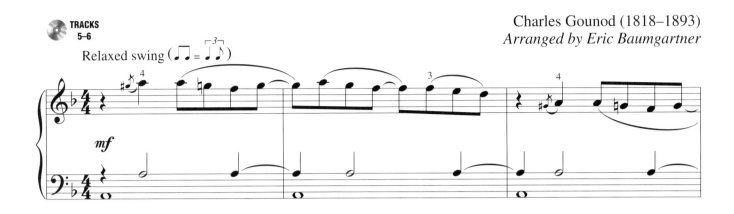

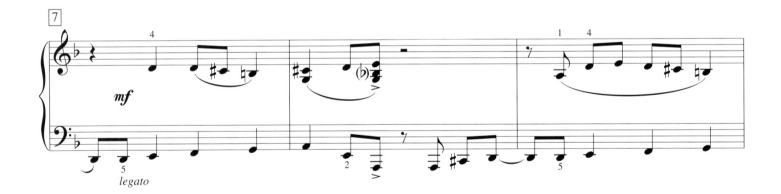

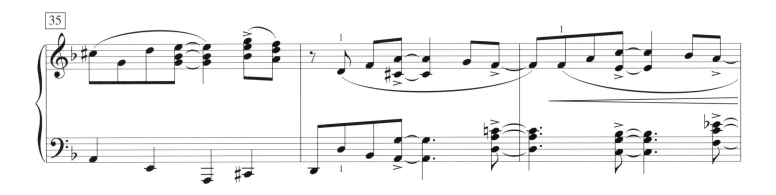

Spinning Song

Albert Ellmenreich (1816–1905)
Arranged by Eric Baumgartner

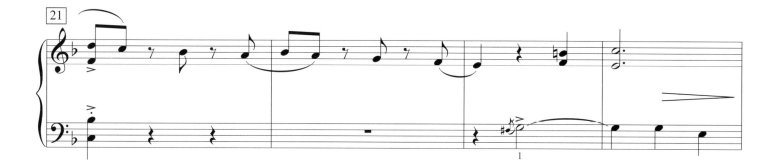

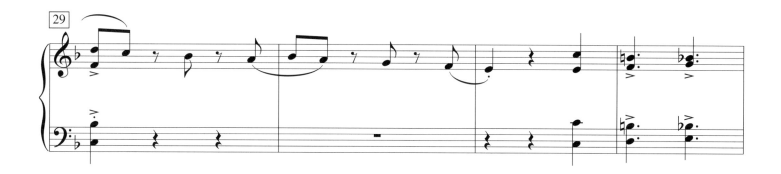

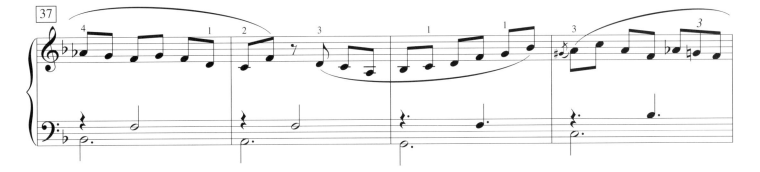

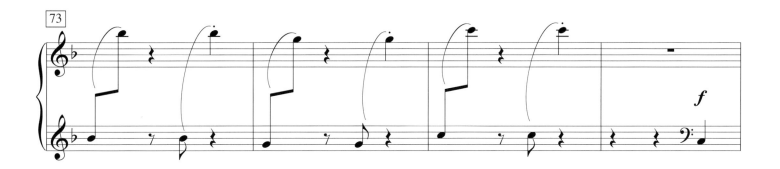

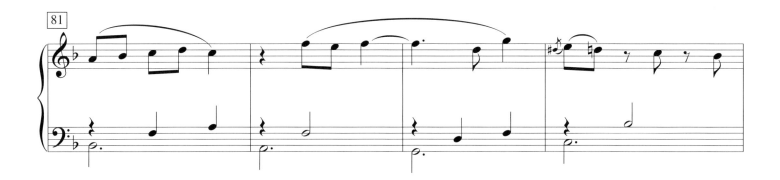

Song for the New World

Antonín Dvořák (1841–1904)
Arranged by Eric Baumgartner

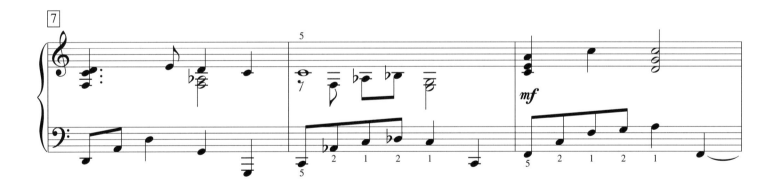

Symphonic Swing
(Theme from *Symphony No. 40*)

Wolfgang Amadeus Mozart (1756–1791)
Arranged by Eric Baumgartner

TRACKS 11–12

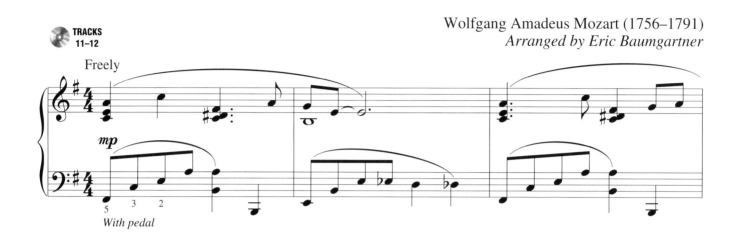

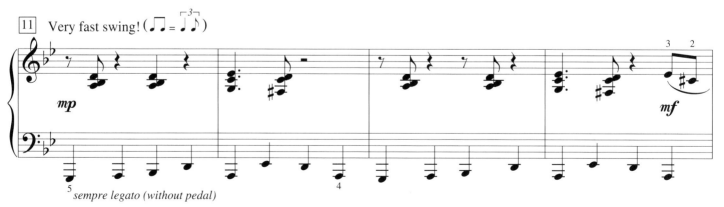

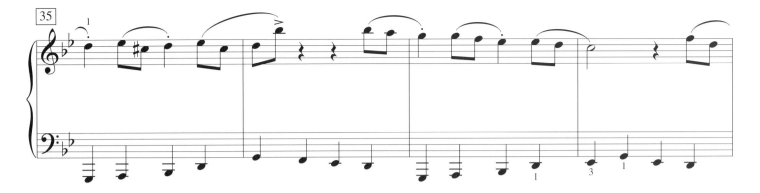

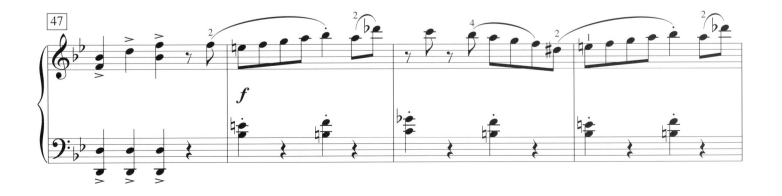

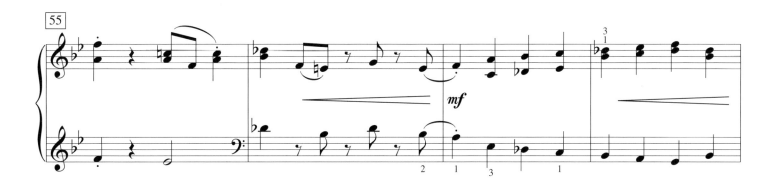

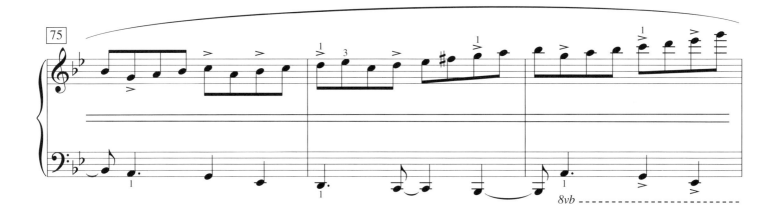

Eric Baumgartner's *Jazz It Up! Series* are wonderful jazz arrangements of well-known tunes that both experienced and beginning pianists will enjoy. The stylized pieces are intentionally written without chord symbols or improvisation sections, although pianists are encouraged to experiment and explore!

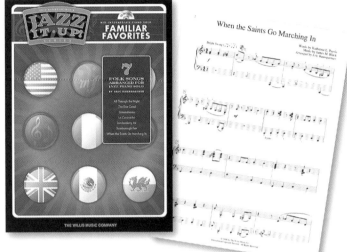

Jazz It Up! – Christmas
Mid-Intermediate Level
Deck the Hall • God Rest Ye Merry, Gentlemen • O Christmas Tree • The Coventry Carol • Good King Wenceslas • Jingle Bells.
00416752 Book/CD $9.95

Jazz It Up! – Familiar Favorites
SEVEN FOLK SONGS
Mid-Intermediate Level
All Through the Night • The Erie Canal • Greensleeves • La Cucaracha • Londonderry Air • Scarborough Fair • When the Saints Go Marching In.
00416778 Book/CD $9.95

Jazz It Up! – Classics
Mid-Intermediate Level
Funeral March of a Marionette (Gounod) • Habanera (Bizet) • Nutcracker Rock (Tchaikovsky) • Song for the New World (Dvořák) • Spinning Song (Ellmenreich) • Symphonic Swing (Mozart).
00416867 Book/CD $9.99

WILLIS MUSIC

EXCLUSIVELY DISTRIBUTED BY

HAL•LEONARD® CORPORATION

7777 W. BLUEMOUND RD. P.O. BOX 13819 MILWAUKEE, WI 53213

Prices, contents, and availability
subject to change without notice.

0310